# MIDDLE EAST
## DIARIES

*Walking the Ancient Paths*

MIRJAM JOHNSON

# CONTENTS

To Yahweh, my Father and my God, I owe You everything.
You granted my life as a prize, wherever I went.


*This is what the LORD says:*
*"Stand at the crossroads and look; ask for the ancient paths,*
*ask where the good way is, and walk in it,*
*and you will find rest for your souls."*
*Jeremiah 6:16, NIV*

# FOREWORD

The travels that are described in Mirjam's book are quite amazing and somewhat unbelievable. Today these travels would be impossible because of all the changes that have happened throughout the world since then. It shows that God was watching over Mirjam her whole life. Throughout this book, God will show you that He sends out His disciples by faith. This is what Jesus showed us by saying,

*"Provide neither gold nor silver nor copper in your money belts, nor bag for your journey, nor two tunics, nor sandals, nor staffs; for a worker is worthy of his food" (Matthew 10: 9, 10).*

We are called just as the disciples were. It is not required that we have a formal education, nor a ministry, nor even a lot of money to go. We are called to go only with our faith. May God speak to you when you read about Mirjam's travels with the Lord.

Christopher Johnson, Mirjam's husband

# INTRODUCTION

When I was a little girl, my mother would read from the family Bible every day after Dinner. I remember the Israelite stories of desert struggles and wars to enter the Promised Land. In my childlike mind I was thinking my mother was reading our family's history. I remember the longing to connect to that old family that God had connected Himself with. When I was a little older, I watched *"Lawrence of Arabia"* on our TV one day. The movie, a seven times Academy Awarded epic film, is about Officer T.E. Lawrence traveling the Middle East during World War I. Ever since then it was as if God imprinted a love for the Middle East in my soul. I always had a longing to go, but never knew how it would come about. In the following chapters you will see how God made it happen.

I pray that as you read my book, you will feel inspired to do the things that God put in your heart. He is calling you to live for Him.

Be blessed, be free in the Holy Spirt of God and have fun!

Mirjam

# CHAPTER ONE

# A PRODIGAL'S PILGRIMAGE

It was the year 1999, the year that many thought the Lord Jesus would come back at the turn of the Century. They had based this expectation on the words of the prophet Hosea, where he says, *"Come, and let us return to the LORD; For He has torn, but He will heal us; He has stricken, but He will bind us up. After two days He will revive us; On the third day He will raise us up, that we may live in His sight." Hosea 6:1-2.* The interpretation of the two days representing two thousand years would have been based on Moses's words in Psalm 90 that *"a thousand years in Your sight are like yesterday when it is past."* Or else on Peter his words *"that with the Lord one day is as a thousand years, and a thousand years as one day.*" *2 Peter 3:8.* I was clueless about it all when boarding a plane to Israel. I believed in the God of Israel and the return of the Messiah. But I also knew Jesus' words when He said, *"But of that day and hour no one knows, not even the Angels of Heaven, but My Father only." Watch, therefore, for you do not know what hour your Lord is coming." Matthew 24:36,42.* I didn't know that a visit to Israel would be so life-changing, but I was never more excited in my life than that day in May of 1999, my first visit to the Promised Land!

The way this trip came about is an absolute grace of God story. I was 26 years of age and in my most prodigal time of life. Maybe you have been there too. It is not that you deny your faith in God, but your need for love and purpose in life is pulling you into your flesh and getting the best of you. Perhaps if I was married it would have been a different story, but I was not. I may have had the chance earlier in life to marry someone, but I was always afraid to commit myself. I knew deep down inside that it wasn't what I should do, but I also didn't know what else I should be doing! What struggle it was! Perhaps you are in it right now as you read this book. Hang in there. You may find some clues to your calling as you read along. I pray God will speak to you throughout my book. *"Thus says the LORD: "Stand in the ways and see, and ask for the old paths, where the good way is, and walk in it; then you will find rest for your souls." Jer.6:16.*

So here I am, going to Israel by myself. The only thing I had was a name and a phone number of a Dutch-Israeli family whom I had never met before. It was really God who led me that way, yet I was oblivious. Let me tell you how this came about.

Back in Holland, I was working in the University Medical Center as a Microbiological Laboratory Technician. I commuted each day but wanted to live closer to the Hospital where I worked. Finding living space in a city with thousands of students is not an easy task. I responded to an ad in the paper where a room was offered in a shared house. I made a call and talked to the homeowner, only to find out that the house was guys-only. But somehow strangely the homeowner called me back a little later. He told me that he hoped he wasn't making a mistake, but that he felt he should give me the room. I moved in a week later. The guys were all very nice to me, some became good friends. Of course, they were doing all kinds of partying and crazy stuff. Putting an ignorant small-town girl in a big city is asking for trouble. But I have already told you that God met me in my most prodigal time of life. After a year or so living there, one of the guys, seeing that I didn't know what to do with my vacation time, proposed that I'd go visit his sister in Israel. His sister had married a Jewish man and was living in the Tel Aviv area. It sounded good to me, so that is how I ended up in Israel in May of 1999. It was beyond excitement to fly to the Promised Land!

When the plane landed everyone clapped their hands in honor of the pilot's landing skills. Since it was my very first flight,

I thought that was common. But I found out later that it was an Israeli tradition. I loved it! After going through the airport's customs, the family picked me up and brought me to their home in Kiryat Ono. Coming from a country where the skies are mostly overcast, going to Israel with its Mediterranean climate, sunshine and bright blue skies was fabulous! I had my first experience with a Kabbalat Shabbat dinner and saw how Jewish people live their faith. It was all so awesome to me and special! After a few days exploring Tel Aviv, it was time for another place to explore. They told me there was a bus stop in their neighborhood with buses going to Jerusalem. I was so excited, off I went. I carried a small backpack, a guidebook, and enough shekels to spend some nights in Jerusalem.

# CHAPTER TWO

# JERUSALEM! JERUSALEM!

My mother grew up in a devout Christian family with eight siblings. Her father and all her siblings played musical instruments. My mother played the harmonica and organ. Growing up we had an organ in our house and she would play hymns on it and sing. I remember my mother would play "The Holy City" on the organ. And when she would sing the famous chorus, I would feel something stirring inside my spirit. *"Jerusalem, Jerusalem, lift up your gates and sing, hosanna in the highest, hosanna to the King."* As the bus neared Jerusalem, those words were reverberating in my soul. I could hardly believe I was about to enter Jerusalem! The Holy City, where our Lord was crucified! It was beyond anything I could ever imagine!

The bus stopped at the Damascus Gate in the Old City of Jerusalem. It is the area where most Arabs live. If you have never been to Israel, I will explain a little. Jerusalem is divided into four quarters, though there are no real infrastructural dividing lines. There is the Muslim quarter, the Jewish quarter, the Christian quarter, and the Armenian quarter. But it wasn't always like that. We know from the Bible that David conquered Jerusalem and made it Israel's eternal capital around 1000 BC. If you have never read it, you can find this account in 2 Samuel 5. It's hard to believe when you walk into a city that makes you feel like you're stepping into history. Like any place in the Middle East, it was also very crowded with people. Visiting several Biblical sites in Jerusalem to any Christian is just extremely special. But when God is meeting with you in Jerusalem, that is beyond expectation! I will get to that story a little later. I only had eight days on this trip and went to visit the Galilee as well. I remember a conversation I had with another tourist. We both sort of envied the people of Israel, who were living out their faith in strong communities. We people of the West find ourselves assimilated into the secular world.

Once I was back in Tel Aviv, the family asked me if I wanted to go to a wedding with a neighbor friend. I remember thinking, a wedding?! I felt so unprepared! I didn't have a proper dress to wear. I had brought one dress and asked the sisters of the family if that was okay to wear. In my ignorance I did not know what cultural experience I was embarking on. I felt so insecure that I almost didn't dare to go. Everyone knew what they were doing, except for me. But I got over my fear and went anyway! It was a Yemenite Jewish wedding of large proportions. I wondered if wedding feasts get any bigger outside of Israel. It's like half the country shows up! But it was a great celebration of marriage, with hundreds of people, buffets of food, music, dancing, and a traditional wedding ceremony that was gorgeous. I snapped so many pictures that night, it was an amazing cultural experience.

When it was time to leave Israel, I did not want to leave. I had a sense of belonging there, of homecoming that I could not explain. I remember talking to my friends about it and they jokingly told me I could come back and join the IDF (the Israeli Army). I left the country with five pounds of cucumbers and tomatoes. Those flavorful vegetables never taste better than in Israel. To this day, I still don't know why they let me on the plane with so many vegetables, but the favor of God was on me.

---

# Chapter Three

# TWO MIRACLES!

I was still working in the Hospital, and upon my return I realized that I did not feel the same. Several of my co-workers were vying for supervisor positions or research spots that paid more money. I just had none of those ambitions. I could not get Israel out of my mind. There was also a deep pull for freedom inside of me. By the Divine providence of God, I had a ton of extra vacation days. The year prior we had merged two Laboratories, which meant a lot of overtime hours. Unlike in the USA where you simply get paid for your overtime, in Holland you can choose to have your hours paid or your time returned. I chose to have my overtime hours returned. It added up to 20 days, so I planned another trip to Israel in October 1999 for several weeks. I bought myself a backpacker guide to the Middle East and planned to visit Jordan as well as

Egypt's Sinai desert. Mind you this was 1999, before the second Intifada and there was a lot more freedom to travel into historical areas.

This time in Jerusalem, to learn more about the history, I decided to book a tour with Zion Walking Tours. They still exist today, and can be found in the Old City's Jaffa Gate area. I toured the Old historical city with a group of people and became instant friends with a Jewish American girl called Pella. Since Jerusalem has been destroyed about nineteen times in History, there are many archeological layers to explore. The tour was geared towards the rooftops, the main streets, and the tunnels. It was awesome and all so special to me to walk these Bible-time streets. However, halfway through the three-hour tour, I started to have a rapidly increasing pain in one of my molars. I had quite some dental work done in my life, so I started to get worried something was wrong. Maybe I needed a Dentist, but what would I do in a foreign country? My newly made friend Pella said to me, "Hey Mirjam, what's wrong, your face has changed!" I told her about my ailment. At this point, we were touring the tunnels that lead up to the Western Wall where the Temple of Solomon once stood. The tour guide was explaining how Jewish people often write prayers and stick them in the cracks of the rocks. I was in a time of my life where I wasn't engaged in much prayer, but somehow, I got inspired. At the next stop of our tour, I found a piece of paper in my bag and wrote my prayer on it, asking God to take the toothache away. I stuck it in one of the stone's crevices and went on with the tour. By the time we got to the end of the beautiful walking tour, I realized that the pain was gone! It was a miracle! God met me there in my simple faith! What grace He has for us!

After Jerusalem, I traveled to Eilat with my new friend Pella, whose name means "Marvel of God" in Hebrew. Up to this day, I pay attention to people's names if there is anyone new coming into my life. From the Hebrew perspective, the names of people have purpose and destiny. God was making me marvel at this miracle in Jerusalem! We spent some days in Eilat, which is in the very south of Israel. It's a vacationing town perfect for relaxing and swimming. We snorkeled in the marvelous Red Sea with its beautiful fish and coral reefs. From there I crossed the border into the Sinai desert, which is in Egypt. After a few days with the very friendly Bedouin people, I took a ferry across the Red Sea to Aqaba, which is in Jordan. If you started to wonder how I knew my way around, then here's the answer: *Lonely Planet*. It's a backpackers guidebook written by people who have gone before you and it gives a lot of detailed information on local bus lines, places to stay and areas to avoid. If you ever make it to the beautiful Hashemite Kingdom of Jordan, make sure you visit the Wadi Rum desert and the Nabataean city of Petra.

Coming back to Israel, I wanted to spend the last days of my four-week trip in Galilee and visit some Biblical places. When I checked into a Guesthouse in Tiberias, I met some very nice people from New Zealand. I loved their adventurous spirit, and I joined them on a bike ride around the Sea of Galilee. I joined them for half the trip, but here's what happened next. We stopped at a place called Ein Enov where a waterfall comes down in the Sea of Galilee. It's close to Capernaum, so we decided to make a stop there. The beach and bottom of the lake are all rocks and pebbles. We were all feeling hot from our cycle trip, and cooling off in the water was such a delight. I was wearing my Teva hiking sandals and kept them on while entering the water. I was walking towards the waterfall when something sharp stung the bottom of my right foot. I lifted my foot out of the water and a piece of thick glass had pierced through my sandal into the bottom of my foot! I was bleeding, and I thought to myself, "What do I do now?" My "Kiwi" friends were having fun at the waterfall, taking pictures, and so on. I wandered off a little on my own like a wounded dog, wondering what I should do. Then all of a sudden, my thoughts changed. And I remembered how Jesus would have walked on the water here. And thoughts came to me that if Jesus had walked on these waters, then they must be holy and therefore my foot would be healed! I know it sounds crazy, but I never even prayed! It was just faith from Heaven that fell on me. By the time we got back on our bicycles, I looked at my foot. Not only had it stopped bleeding, but I didn't even see a scar! Up until this day, I still can't believe it. But it's true! Mind you, I was 27 years old and had never seen or heard any modern-day miracles. Later in my life, after I joined Pentecostal circles, I was exposed to many more miracles and divine healings. I didn't even know there was a whole lot of doctrine behind the fathers of the Reformation, who were believing that miracles ceased with the Apostles and the First Church. I learned that later. But at that time of my life, no one around me even talked about God or Jesus outside of Church, let alone told me they had a Divine experience. But I know God met me there in Israel and it was very special to me.

I parted from my New Zealand friends and cycled back to Tiberias along the beautiful Sea of Galilee. I remember several cars going by and honking at me. I couldn't figure out if it was because I was a girl or because people got scared of me driving my bike on a highway. Either way, I kept cycling till I got back to Tiberias. My second Middle East trip had come to an end and I felt so sad that I had to leave again. But God had a plan!

# CHAPTER FOUR

# NEW AGE CURIOSITY

When I was back in the Lab, my co-workers wanted to know how my trip had been to the Middle East. I remember saying to several of them, "My next trip is going to be a one-way." I didn't even know what I meant by that! But something inside of me was changing. I felt more disconnected from my own country and more drawn to the Middle East. It was God's doing, but I had no clue. I made a plan to save up as much money as I could and then hand in my resignation eight months later, June 2000. I know it sounds crazy. But, at least once in your life, you have to make a decision that goes against the grain. I was never happier in my life. Knowing that I would be able to travel more and be free. Perhaps I was looking for identity and purpose. Ultimately, I was looking for God, but I didn't know it. As a Protestant Christian, I never really saw examples of people devoting their lives to God and serving Jesus. That was something Catholics did. The two people who inspired me as a young girl were Jeanne D'Arc, the French martyr, and Iet Bleeker. The latter was a lady who would visit our Church on our annual Israel Sunday. She was Dutch but had lived in Jerusalem since the 1950s, working for a Christian Ministry. Listening to her stories from Israel was always so intriguing to me as a little girl. God was planting seeds in my heart, that He could pick the fruits from later in my life.

Before I go on about my Middle East adventures, I want to tell you a story that led me to a new kind of spiritual awakening!

Let me explain a little first. God made us body, spirit, and soul. And there is the Holy Spirit of God, given to those who believe in Christ Jesus. Evil spirits, however, come from the powers of darkness. These are the 'agents' of Satan that we deal with on this earth. Spirits of darkness often know more about people, than the people of God! (I wrote more about the supernatural in my book called, "Ten Waves of Awe".) So, back when I was in my twenties and hungry for spiritual experiences, I went to a New Age Fair one day with a friend from work. The Fair displayed every type of New Age practice and had booths with Astrologists, Energy healers and Fortune tellers that you could visit. My friend wanted to go see this guy who was a type of fortune teller. She sat with him at the table and the man spoke several things to her. I kept my distance somewhat to give her privacy. When she was done, she got up and said to me, "Now it's your turn." I made a few steps toward the table when all sudden the man started yelling at me, "You know who you are! I don't want to talk to you!"

It was a demonic spirit in that man, who saw the Holy Spirit in me. It was crazy! I kind of laughed at it thinking, "Okay, I know who I am and I probably don't need to be here." And I told my friend I wanted to leave. I didn't know then what I know now. The people of God should never dabble in New Age practices because it invites demonic spirits into their lives. Of course, no one tells you it is demonic because the devil is a master liar and deceiver. They will tell you it's guiding spirits, or "energy" or even "your angels". But let me tell you, the so-called "guiding spirits" will turn against you and tear you to pieces. I will share something about that later.

When the eight months of saving up money came to an end, I handed in my resignation at the Hospital. My co-workers organized a goodbye Party for me at a Middle Eastern Restaurant. Several colleagues shared some loving words. We were always a great team at the Lab. One of the Doctors shared with us that he didn't understand why I did this, but that it fitted me because I was always the 'odd bird' among the workers. I took that as a compliment. Dutch people are painfully honest at times.

I ended the lease of my apartment, sold, and gave away furniture, and put my personal belongings in my dad's attic. I bought a one-way ticket to Athens for sixty Dutch Guilders. I planned to travel from Greece to Turkey and then just go where the wind blew me. Finally, I had bought my freedom. I never felt happier in my life. Middle East, here I come again!

# CHAPTER FIVE

# WITHIN THE CITY OF ISTANBUL

After spending a few days exploring Athens and the island of Samos, I took a ferry to the West coast of Turkey. Turkish people are extremely hospitable. They have a beautiful country and a rich heritage. It's very sad that a lot of the Middle Eastern countries are known for their notorious regimes, extremism, or violence because the majority of people in those nations are beautiful people. I took a trip to Ephesus, an ancient city from Roman times. I remember the tour guide speaking about John the Apostle, and I felt such a draw to find traces of my Christian faith. When I made it to Istanbul, I planned to stay there for a while to apply for travel visas. I went to the Syrian Embassy to apply for a travel visa and then to the Iranian Embassy to do the same. As a woman you will have to dress modestly according to their dress code, and so I did. While I waited several weeks for these visa applications to be processed, I worked in the Guesthouse where I was staying. I had heard from other travelers that obtaining a tourist visa to Iran was often rejected, depending on the relations with your native country. And if you got in, then the authorities would decide how long your stay was. So I had to wait and see if they would grant me entrance.

Istanbul, formerly known as Constantinople, is a beautiful city, especially the oldest part of the city called Sultan Ahmet, west of the Bosphorus. The Guesthouse was located right across from the famous Aya Sophia, one of the oldest remaining Churches in the world, built by Emperor Justinian in the 6th Century. However, it is believed that the original Church on the site was built by Constantine himself in the year 325. It was the time when the Romans stopped persecuting Christians and made Christianity their "legal" faith. Fast forward to the 15th Century, when the Turks conquered Constantinople and transformed the Aya Sophia into a Mosque. They added minarets and other Islamic relics, but you can still see the Christian mosaics. It is almost as if you can sense the presence of God in that place. I visited numerous famous ancient Churches throughout my travels, but none is like it.

I was sharing a room with a lady who taught English at an International School in Istanbul. She was a Christian and told me something incredible one day. Mind you, I was looking for spirituality in the wrong places but didn't know it. We went out to eat one day together, and then she told me a story about her family. She shared how they were into witchcraft and how it nearly killed her when she refused to partake. Very strong spirits were operating in her family line and I wondered how she got out of it. Then she told me about the power of Christ, and how He saved her and set her free. I had never heard such a story! She also told me she had seen that I was interested in these New Age practices and carried certain "lucky charms". She told me I was walking into dangerous territory. I appreciated her speaking so boldly and caring about me. I had never thought about it being dangerous, but deep down inside I knew she spoke the truth! I will tell you later what I did with the book and the charms I carried. For now, I will finish my story about my time in Istanbul.

Working in a Guesthouse where travelers come from all over the world is a fun thing to do. After a few weeks I went back to the Iranian Embassy, again in full covering. The people at the Embassy were so friendly, and when they gave me back my Passport, I found out that they had granted me a Tourist visa for two weeks. I was so excited! Now I had another ancient land to explore.

I was about to leave Istanbul to see other Turkish places of interest before crossing over into Iran. Because of new guests arriving, I had to change rooms in the Guesthouse. When I opened my window, there was the Aya Sophia only a few yards across the car-free street. One night I woke up from a very deep peaceful sleep and I knew I had heard Angels singing, they sounded like monks. I was stunned! Maybe they were still stationed at that beautiful ancient Church, and God let me hear their songs.

A few days later I was on a ten-hour night bus down south to Fethiye. Night buses are an adventure in Turkey. The bus driver made a stop somewhere at 3 a.m. to get the bus washed. I just wanted to get some sleep! In the Western part of Turkey, I always felt safe. In the East, it was a different story, but I will get to that later. The south of Turkey is on the blessed and beautiful Mediterranean Sea. It was here that God showed up again for me.

# CHAPTER SIX

# THE GREAT SEA AND CAPPADOCIA

I settled in Fethiye, which is a backpacker's hub for day-trips in the area. Turkey was once part of the Greek Empire before the Romans took over, and there are lots of amazing archeological sites to see. I joined some other backpackers on a boat trip to do some island hopping. Part of the coast is rugged with mountains, forests, and beaches. One day I went into the woods where no one would see me. I took my new age book and "lucky charms" and burned it all up. I can't remember if I prayed or not, but I just sat there looking at the fire when suddenly I felt something leave me, like a spirit. It was as if a dark veil had come off me. I looked around the woods and I saw trees I had not seen before! I saw all kinds of fruit trees with fruit on it. I thought this must be like the Garden of Eden! I don't know if that was an earthly experience or a heavenly one, but I felt so much rest in my soul. I knew I had done the right thing; there would be no more New Age superstition faith for me! True enlightening comes from the God Who made heaven and earth. That reminds me of a story I heard some years ago. A woman was sharing how she grew up with a nanny, who would take her to Satanic meetings. There she was dedicated to Satan when she was a young girl. She didn't know any other faith and was bound to darkness for many years. I will fast-forward the story. In her early twenties, she got out of the coven and fled to a Christian Spirit-filled woman. By surrendering her life to God, she was set free by the power of Jesus. She then described that it was the first time in her life that she could hear birds singing. Wow! That is what dark spirits do, they make you blind and deaf for the beauty of God's creation! I experienced a little of that coming out of the deception. I felt hope and joy again. It was as if a curse was broken over my life. So, with renewed faith, I went on with my travels.

All the Churches that Jesus mentions in the Book of Revelation are in present-day Turkey. It was the place where the first Christians found refuge from persecution. I was able to visit the area called Cappadocia in mid-Turkey, where Christians lived in cave-like structures. We read in the book of Acts that Cappadocians were in Jerusalem during the day of Pentecost.

After Cappadocia, I explored some places in Eastern Turkey. Mind you I was perhaps ignorant of any dangers, but God in His grace always protected me. I discovered that in some places a woman traveling alone meant she was a prostitute, and therefore despised. Some people turned very hostile and one man even spit at me. I didn't stay there very long.

I arrived in a place called Doğubeyazıt, which some Americans jokingly called "Dog Biscuit." It borders with Iran, and there you can see Mount Ararat. The Mountain is believed to be the landing place for the Ark of Noah. You can find this story in the book of Genesis chapter 8. When I was there, they had it all fenced off and no tourist was allowed even near the fence. They were doing archeological digs in the surrounding area of the boat's frame. Amazingly enough the remains of the boat's framework fit the 300-cubits long and 50-cubits-wide Ark that Noah built. The Bible researcher and explorer Ron Wyatt describes finding an ancient altar, which would have been another piece of evidence of Noah's existence. Nowadays it is open to the public and guided tours can take you around the Ark's resting place.

I had to go shopping for new clothes before crossing the border into Iran. And then the day came that I took a shared taxi to the border crossing in my new chador. There was a big hall with lots of people and a somewhat chaotic atmosphere, but I made it through to the other side!

# CHAPTER SEVEN

# ANCIENT PERSIA

The first place I stayed in Iran was Tabriz. It was July by now and very hot. I would go out and walk the streets and see women walking along the buildings to find shade. Wearing the black chador with covered head made it hard to move around at first. But after a few days, I got more accustomed. At the time of this writing Iran has been under strict Islamic rule for 45 years. For women showing half of their hair or skin is punishable by religious laws. As soon as the locals noticed I was a tourist they would come up to me and say, "I'm sorry you have to dress like this." Sometimes even a whole group of people would gather around me as if I were a celebrity. People were curious to meet foreigners and were extremely friendly. I often met local people who would want to show me around their city. I had a little Farsi language book which came in extremely handy because not everyone spoke English. When I would travel to another city, the people would often shuffle seats around so I could sit next to a woman. And then as the trip took off, they offered me the food they brought. I never felt more special than in the country formerly known as Persia. I pretty much traveled alone for the two weeks I had, but God always brought other travelers alongside me when I needed it. I spent several days in the beautiful city of Isfahan, and there I found a fellow traveler who had made a local friend. The Iranian friend invited us to come to his home. I thought about what to do with this invitation but decided to go along. Little did I know that the man's home and family were six hours away amid the Zagros Mountains! We took bus after bus with lots of people on board as well as their merchandise, vegetables, or carpets. It was quite a cultural change. The Zagros Mountains stretch across the west side of Iran, and they border with Iraq as well. The ancient city of Shushan, or Susa is on the south end of the area. Persian Kings like Darius, Xerxes, and Ahasuerus ruled from here. It is where many of the exiled Jews lived in the times of Esther, Ezra, and Nehemiah.

After we transferred several buses, we walked about an hour over the barren mountains, and deep into the countryside. While we traveled, I quickly drew a map in my notebook. I added names of places I saw on signs, asking locals where we were, because I started to lose track of where we were heading. Once we arrived at the family's home, I realized I had gone back in time a hundred years. The family lived in a small stone house in the country with no running water or electricity. They grew wheat and other crops. It was an agricultural but dry landscape. Obviously, in Summer it does not rain in the Middle East. Our new friend Mohammed had four younger sisters. They all flocked around me and served me as if I was a princess. When it was getting dark, the men came home from working the land and we all ate together on a spread-out cloth on the floor. After Dinner it was bedtime. Mattresses were rolled out on the floors. Women and girls stay and sleep together in one room and boys do the same. When I took my chador off and my headscarf, they all marveled at my blonde hair and offered to brush it. There was no English at all so I had to use the Farsi words I learned. After a few days with the family, the time came to leave. I carried several silver bracelets and other jewelry and was able to give each of the girls a little gift. What a hospitable family they were. I felt like I had stepped back into the times of Abraham, where travelers were treated like honorable guests. They hand-sifted their wheat and loaded it on a donkey to carry. They hand-cut crystalized sugar as well. It made me appreciate my rich life even more so.

I visited one more ancient place in Iran before heading back to the Turkish border. It was called Bam, and it is one of the most ancient intact places in the Middle East. I don't know how it looks now because I visited there in the year 2000. Bam's modern city was hit with a devastating earthquake in 2003, which killed around 26.000 people. The old sandcastle-looking city is now one of UNESCO's World Heritage sites and lies on the ancient Silk Road. It is near the border with Pakistan in the southeastern part of Iran. The guesthouse where I stayed had several date palms. The owner would lay a cloth under the tree, and then shake it fervently so that the dates would drop. He would then collect the dates, wash them in water, and give them to us to eat. The new city, like almost any border town I visited, hosted some strange and illegal trade. God always protected me from wicked people who do their evil deeds in the dark. I can't help but think that's why the earthquake hit the town so badly. God is just and he hears the cry of His people.

# CHAPTER EIGHT

# KURDISTAN

When my two weeks of Iranian adventures ended, I crossed the border back into Turkey and planned to stay in Van. My travel plan was to visit a couple of places in South East Turkey before heading into neighboring Syria. This area of Turkey is mostly inhabited by Kurdish people. They have been in long-standing conflicts with the Turkish, feeling oppressed and discriminated. After the First World War the Allies and the League of Nations drew the borders in the Middle East, and some tribes were left without a name for their homeland. The Kurdish people are one of those. They live in East Turkey, North Iraq, West Iran, and North Syria. And now I had entered their homeland. Some call it Kurdistan, others call it East Turkey. I have no opinion on the matter but am reminded of Jesus His words, when He predicted in Matthew 24 that, *"Na-*

*tion shall rise against Nation.*" Nation is coming from the Greek word *Ethnos,* meaning people groups or ethnicities. In the same prophetic utterance, Jesus also talked about *"wars and rumors of wars"*, which have been happening in the world in the last 2000 years.

As I was walking the streets still in my chador, a jovial non-Turkish guy started talking to me. He was with a couple of others and asked me if I had come from Iran. I soon found out they were Yugoslavs; Slovenians to be precise. So, I ended up tagging along with them for several days. We wanted to visit the same places, so it worked out great. And since this area was less safe for a woman alone, God had provided protection again through fellow backpackers. One of them was a tour guide, using their trip to scout out several places for a future organized tour. We climbed a volcano together and stayed with a Kurdish family. The locals lived kind of like the family I stayed with in Iran. Except they had herds of sheep and goats. The daughters of the family took me to their pastures to milk the animals, and showed me how they make their delicious yogurts and cheese. These people were Muslims but not as religiously strict. The more south we traveled the more sense I had of walking in ancient paths. We found a place where you could swim in the Euphrates River, by just jumping in with your clothes on. Later we stationed ourselves in Sanliurfa, a beautiful old city, and from there we visited Haran, the city of the Patriarchs. Abraham's father Terah took his family there first, when they left Chaldea. They dwelt many years in Haran until God called Abram to go to Canaan. Later in Hebrew history Jacob went to live with his uncle Laban, who still lived in Haran. The city has ancient mud-dome houses you can visit. It is amazing to visit these historical Biblical places.

The last stop in Turkey was Antakya, a crossroads city between the ancient Anatolia region and the Middle East. It was known in antiquity as Antioch. My tour guide friend told me how the Apostle Paul and Barnabas parted ways here when they were preaching the Gospel. Antioch was the place where the Apostles sent the Jerusalem decree, exempting new believers in Christ from being circumcised. I wasn't preaching the Gospel yet, but I did part ways with my Yugoslav friends and got on a bus to Allepo.

I had become good friends with the Slovenians that God had sent my way. It was safer for me to travel with them. After I left the Middle East, they invited me to visit their country. You can find that story later in this book.

# CHAPTER NINE

# THE ROAD TO DAMASCUS

I was traveling alone again, but now to another ancient country: Syria. My journey there did not start very well. I had eaten some contaminated food the night before in Turkey and was now dealing with a severe case of food poisoning. It was so bad that I had a fever and was emptied on every side. I laid on a bed in a women's dorm all day feeling terrible, not knowing what to do except drink water. Then a lady came in with long silver hair. She was the first one that took notice of me. She then told me I should boil some rice, not drain the water, and add some garlic to it. So I got up, though I had very little energy, and went to the market to buy those items. After I cooked it and ate it, I laid down again to rest. The next thing I knew was that the fever was gone and I was cured! It was an absolute miracle. I found out a week later that my Yugoslav friend, who had eaten the same food, had ended up in the Hospital being completely dehydrated. God had sent another Angel to take care of me!

From Allepo I traveled to a couple of other places in Syria. One of them was Palmyra, another UNESCO World Heritage Site. It is an ancient trade route city that was set in an oasis in the desert. I found some fellow backpackers and went to explore the monumental ruins of the city when the sun was rising. I made some stunning pictures as you can imagine!

I still don't know why I did this, but I decided to hitch a ride to Damascus from Palmyra. I figured there was only one road to go, and the three-hour trip through the desert would be easy. It did not take long before a small truck picked me up. There was a driver and a passenger with a leg injury. Syrians are very friendly and hospitable. However, at some point, they started talking and pointing to the man's hurting leg. He needed my seat to prop up his leg, so they stopped the truck and let me out. I was stunned! There were no other vehicles around, and I found myself "in the middle of nowhere." Other than that, it was soaring hot, and I only had half a bottle of water left. But thank God that I was wearing a sunhat. I laughed at myself and had faith that someone else would soon show up. You might shake your head at me at this point I understand. But I was always drawn to the desert, and its absolute serenity away from the motorized world. It calmed me in ways I had never felt before. I didn't pray, but I knew God was with me, so I just kept walking at the side of the road. I remember coming to a junction where the left turn would take you to Baghdad. I was still hundreds of miles away from Damascus, but I kept on walking. After about half an hour another truck came by and stopped. This man motioned me to get in and he let me ride with him. I thanked him many times in my best Arabic. He spoke no English, but was extremely friendly. He seemed very determined to get me to Damascus safely. Perhaps he too was an Angel of the Lord. When we reached the outskirts of Damascus, he got out and even paid for my bus ride to the center of the city. What a wonderful Syrian! I was so joyful!

When I arrived at the guesthouse, I saw a few familiar faces, backpackers that I had met in Palmyra. To stretch my budget, I bargained with the guesthouse owner about the price of lodging. He looked at my Passport and then laughed and said, "Oh, it's you, the bargaining queen." He had heard about me from other travelers. I just felt so joyful all the time; It must have been God's Angels surrounding me. I had a sense of destiny and peace over me that I had not felt before.

Damascus, the Old City, is very special. It was founded in the Third millennium B.C., but some believe it's older than that. A Street called Straight runs from the east to the west through the old City. Even Jesus knew about this street because in Acts 9:11 He tells Ananias to go see Paul who was staying at the house of Judas on a street called 'Straight'. It was there that Paul got his vision back and spent some time with Jesus' disciples, whom he had first planned to kill! Paul started to preach about Jesus being the Son of God in the Synagogue. He confounded the Jews of Damascus in Acts 9 and they plotted to kill him. But they found out and then lowered Paul in a large basket by night to escape the city. There is a Church called *"Kanisat Mar Bawlus"* or Saint Paul's Chapel, that commemorates these events. I felt enormously privileged to visit that place in the beautiful ancient city of Damascus.

After my application, I was given a 48-hour travel visa to go to Lebanon. Since my time was limited, I thought I would only visit Beirut. When I got off the bus, some local people toured me around, and took me to eat. Somehow as if I had bodyguards assigned to me, I was never left on my own. Everyone was extremely hospitable. Walking on the boulevard along the Mediterranean Sea made me think of my days in Tel Aviv. It looked so similar! Lebanon has beautiful mountains, and their national flag has an evergreen tree on it. The country is mentioned many times in the Bible. Jesus even visited it! *"He went to the region of Tyre and Sidon,"* it says in Matthew 15:21. It was there where He healed a woman's daughter from demon possession. It was a remarkable story of one woman's faith! I could not visit those ancient Biblical cities because my visa was running out of time.

One of the people that helped me find my way in Beirut was working for a prominent Lebanese official. The next day he showed up with a long luxurious limousine to take me to the bus station for my bus back to Damascus. I laughed so hard when I saw that. It was crazy. I do not recommend copying this trip if you're a girl reading this book. The world has changed a lot since then.

After Beirut and my return to Damascus, I didn't know where else to go anymore. I was done traveling and needed to settle myself somewhere. The desire to improve my English was rising in me, and I considered settling in England. I flew out of Syria back to Istanbul to meet up for a few days with my Yugoslav friends. They went back home, and I boarded a plane to London. I was sad to leave my beloved Middle East behind me, but deep down inside I knew I would be back one day.

# CHAPTER TEN

# EGYPT AND JORDAN

London is one of the biggest European cities I know. I had toured London a few years before. It is pretty amazing but overwhelmingly large. So this time I left for a coastal place called Brighton. At this point in my life, I just needed to reflect on everything that I had experienced in the Middle East. I didn't know what God had planned for me next, but I remember missing that connection to Him. I was back in the "busy Western World". After working several odd jobs in the English coastal town, someone told me about a job at American Express. The European Head Office of American Express was based in Brighton. Someone I knew set me up for an interview, and I was hired on the spot because I could speak Dutch and German. It was the favor of God for sure! My main goal for staying in the UK was to improve my English, and make money so I could travel some more. I worked many hours and saved up my British pounds. Rental spaces are scarce in the UK, and prices are high, therefore I rented a small room in a shared house. I also made some new friends. The room I paid for in the house was jokingly called "the cupboard" because it was so small. I bought myself a used mountain bike for five pounds, and rode many miles up and down the beautiful hills. I had a lot of time to reflect on my Middle Eastern travels, and I eagerly wanted to find a Church to connect to. But somehow, I never did. I had problems connecting to the Western world's ways and religious practices. I always felt most connected to God when being outdoors. And since I rode my bike a lot and would roller skate along the boulevard, I felt quite content. But deep inside I longed to go back to the Middle East and felt an unexplainable draw to Israel. Later in this book, you will see how God brought me back at the appointed time.

My friends in the former Yugoslavia kept asking me when I was going to see their country, so I finally succumbed and took a trip to Slovenia. It was early Spring of 2001, and I made a few attempts to learn skiing. Slovenians are master skiers, and you would see little five-year-olds going down the slopes like adults. It was quite intimidating for a clumsy first-time skier. But there was more to do in the Balkans. My tour-guide friend took me throughout the country, and sometimes I would join his tours. I travelled to all the former Yugoslav republics and learned a lot about their history and culture. All the Yugoslav people have one thing in common: a great sense of humor! I only keep good memories of my time there, and till this day, they are people I hold close to my heart. Later I went down to Kosovo and worked there for a Humanitarian Organization. That region was still in the aftermath of the war, and I worked there mainly with children and widows who were traumatized from the war. I will cut my Balkan time short now and fast-forward the story back to the Middle East. Leaving my good friends in the Balkans left me quite broken inside. In an attempt to get myself back together, I flew to Cairo to meet up with an old friend. I didn't know at the time that this was all God's doing. I had felt forever wrecked by that first trip to Israel in 1999. I had lost the connection to the real purpose of my life, feeling uprooted and displaced. I will tell you what happened next. Here is an excerpt of my book Ten Waves of Awe;

*"I had been a Christian all my life, but my heart was very wounded. I had fallen into a deep dark pit that I could not escape from. Call it depression. I saw no purpose for myself anymore and felt that God had abandoned me. I spent a week in the Sinai desert, trying to get myself together. But whatever I tried, failed. I remember I cried every day and found no comfort. I was staying in a small coastal village, where local Bedouins run some guesthouses. Finally, I decided I would cry out to God in the desert. I went for a long walk, wandering away from the village. I was so desperate to meet God that I thought death was the only solution. So I cried and cried and fell on my knees, begging God to just kill me. I had enough faith to believe God could*

*just let a rock fall on my head and that would be it. I was as dry as the desert itself. But then something supernatural happened! An eagle-type bird appeared high in the sky, and suddenly wind came rushing around me, like a whirlwind. Then an incredible sense of peace came over me and I heard a sound voice saying, "Because you don't see Me, it doesn't mean I'm not there!" That was the very first time I heard God speak to me, like in thoughts. Then as if I was held up in both arms, I was put on my feet and started walking. I know now that God had sent His Angels to help me. I walked very purposefully to someplace in the vast desert but I didn't know where. Then all of the sudden, I saw a stone Well. Yes, it was a very Biblical scene. I looked inside the well, there was no water in it, just darkness. And then I could hear my thoughts, "That's like my life, I am at the bottom of this deep dark pit and I can't get out." Again, I heard God speak very clearly to me, He said, "You have never stretched out your hand to Me to take you out!" That was the revelation of my life! I knew God, I knew Jesus, I knew the Bible. But I never realized that I needed a Savior! You see, I had always been very blessed and self-sufficient. I was also the courageous kind, and all that brought me very far. But I couldn't save my soul. That experience in the desert changed my life forever. It was as if my heart had opened up and I could speak out my hurt, pain, and struggles. I was so stunned by this whole encounter with God that I couldn't speak for a day. I went back to the Bedouin village, got my notebook, and wrote it all down. A few days later I left the village and went to Cairo, where I happened to meet a believer in Christ from Nigeria. I had a little travel Bible in my native language, but she gave me an English Bible. I started reading it and could not stop. The Spirit of God just washed me over with the Word of God. It was an amazing Divine experience that lasted for weeks. At the time I went to an Arabic language school. I would sit on a city bus packed with Muslims, and still read my Bible. I could not think of anything else than the Word of God. One day I read Jesus' words about being born of the Spirit. I was reading it with my new Nigerian friend at the table. I read it and something fell from my eyes, knowing that I needed what Jesus said. I jumped up from my chair and said, "That's what I need, I need a new life!" She was laughing and said she would pray for me. She prayed in her passionate African way and the Holy Spirit came on me. I wept and wept and saw a vision of the Father in Heaven holding out His arms. It was a true prodigal daughter story. And till this day I can still cry about it when I recall it. Surely, I came home that day!*

I saw Jesus in a whole new light. Before He was the Son of God that died on the Cross for our sins. Now, He had become my personal Savior, delivering me from my sin and despair. I found a new purpose! I needed to follow Jesus wherever He told me to go. The Holy Spirit was guiding me in miraculous ways!

After some time back in Cairo, I went with the Nigerian Christian lady to an International Church in Maadi. There she introduced me to a woman called Annemarie Graf, a Dutch missionary to Egypt. It turned out that she was from the North of Holland which was the same area as where I grew up! That was a Divine appointment. Some years later, when Annemarie was retired, I would visit her in Holland sometimes. She spent most of her missionary life in Cairo and would visit the terrible prisons. Later in life, she was honored by the Community Services Association as the *Mother Teresa of Cairo*. She truly was a mother to many lost sons in the Middle East.

Maadi is in the far outskirts of Cairo, which is like a modern city. The inner city of Cairo with the famous Tahrir Square, and ancient *Khan el-Khalili* is a different place. I had taken some Arab lessons and knew the words for left and right but anytime I asked someone in Cairo for directions I always ended up in the wrong place. No one seemed to know their way in this crazy inner city of fifteen million people. The spirit of confusion runs rampant and telling lies seemed to be allowed. Keeping your head clear was a daily work of effort in that city. The endless traffic jams and honking of cars are deafening. I saw people fight on the streets because their cars bumped into each other. People ride bicycles with hundreds of pita loaves piled up on a large wooden board, on top of their heads. (Yes, their heads). Egyptians wave certain hand signs for cities where their buses go. As a tourist you always had to bargain prices for everything, and bargain hard because they would double the price knowing you're a tourist. Once I figured out what the locals paid for something, I would stand my ground in the bargaining process and not pay a penny more, to the frustration of many Egyptians. I loved Egypt and hated it at the same time. I did all the tourist activities, like sailing a Felucca on the Nile River and touring the Giza Pyramids. I explored Luxor with its Valley of the Kings, Karnak, and Aswan in the south. But things did not feel right anymore. I had my encounter with God in the desert, which was amazingly powerful, but now the devil started coming after me.

I traveled with my friend to Siwa in the very western part of Egypt. From there you can visit the 28,000 square mile sand desert that crosses over into Libya. It is called *The Great Sand Sea*. It's really an amazing sight, where those great sand dunes seemed to go on for miles on end. I loved being away from people and noise, but I was hanging out with the wrong person. I believe God had warned me about this man, but I had not fully grasped it. I saw a dark shaded spirit hover over his head one day. I didn't even know I could see demons, but I did. He had some ideas of where we should travel, but we accidentally crossed over into a military zone and some guards started shooting at us, so we had to run away. I started to have a sense something bad was going to happen to me. And I was right. A few days later, some local guy tried to kidnap us, threatening us with a makeshift explosive. It was the scariest thing ever. But here is where God saved me. My friend wanted to hit the kidnapper with something, but I felt strongly in my Spirit we needed to run and not fear his so-called weapon. So we started running with the guy in tow. It could be a scene in a movie for sure. I had no sense of direction as in knowing where we were, but in my Spirit I knew exactly in which direction we should run. It was a supernatural situation at this point. After ten minutes of not seeing a single soul in the vast desert, I heard people talking. We ran to the group of people, and then our attempted kidnapper pretended to be someone else. The language barrier didn't allow the people to understand us, but we were safe and hitched a ride back to the city. It was a crazy time in my life, and I knew I needed to get out of that desert where no one had the fear of God!

After a few days back in Cairo, I felt prompted to visit Jordan again. I traveled to Taba and from there took a ferry to Jordan. After we arrived in Aqaba, I got in a shared taxi. While we were driving out of the city, a Jordanian man in the passenger's seat turned around and started telling me about how He believed in Jesus. Jordan is predominately Muslim, yet this man was as radiant as an Angel of God. He kept on saying that the way to get close to God is to know Jesus and follow Him. I was amazed! I had never met anyone in the Middle East who was as bold as him to share his Christian faith. I took him as a messenger from God and broke away from my friend who had led me into trouble. Let's say I was learning what it means to follow Jesus.

Jordan is a beautiful country with a rich culture and friendly people. After that long drive on a famous ancient desert road called *Kings Highway*, I settled in a little town. God was my "GPS" and never lost me out of His sight. I kept reading my new English Bible.

I was being renewed in my thinking so much by reading the Word of Truth, that I could not stop reading. It sounds funny perhaps, but it was like a spiritual cleansing to me. I was learning about God's love for me and His grace and forgiveness. I had known the Bible all my life, but always dimly as through a veil. Now the Holy Spirit made it come to life and washed me with fresh living water! I was being born again, as Jesus describes in the Gospel of John. Everywhere I traveled in Jordan, I just longed to sit somewhere outside and read my Bible. When I stayed in Amman, the Holy Spirit led me to take a trip to Madaba from where one can climb Mount Nebo. It is the mountain mentioned in Genesis 32 where God showed Moses the promised Land. I was standing outside on the mountain; it was Spring and red poppy flowers bloomed everywhere. When I looked towards Israel, I realized that God had come full circle on a period in my life. I had been given the freedom to travel and live the way I wanted, but now it was time to surrender my life to Him and serve Him. Located on Mount Nebo is a special Byzantine church that was built by Third Century Christians. While inside, I just fell on my knees and prayed. I was humbled by God's presence and promised Him I would serve His people and lead them back to Him the way He had done with me. I wept and prayed for a while. Some other people came in, but I didn't care. As I looked up from the ground, I saw a light coming in that was piercing through the small stained-glass window. The window had an image of Moses with his arms spread open as if giving a blessing. I felt Heaven witnessed my commitment to the Lord, and it was time to leave the Middle East once more.

46

# THE CALLING

Back in Holland, my native country, I worked my old job for several months, filling in people's vacation times. I called a friend one day that I used to work with. Like me, she grew up traditionally Christian but had wandered away from the Lord into the things of this world. On the phone I explained to her that I had a supernatural experience with God in the desert and that I felt He called me to follow Him. Then she shared with me that her sister was going to a Pentecostal Church and how she went one day and felt the same call! So that Summer we went to several Revival meetings where the Holy Spirit had been poured out. We were growing stronger in the knowledge of truth together. In that same season I was baptized, and the Lord cast a demon out of me. You can read that story in my first book. It was a Gospel-type experience that changed the course of my life.

Not long after that I read a very insightful book by Derek Prince, called "They shall expel demons." It was based on Jesus' words. As soon as I picked up that book the Holy Spirit led me in fast, and I found great deliverance from all kinds of demonic forces. It was a Holy Spirit "boot camp" for two weeks straight. I had entered a war with the powers of darkness. But God didn't lead me to defeat but to victory in Christ Jesus! The enemies of God who held me captive in their lies no longer had power over me. I went around and witnessed God's power in my life to anyone who wanted to hear it.

The Hospital let go of me in September that year, as everyone had returned from their vacations. I didn't know what God wanted me to do next. I found a volunteer job in a Christian Bookstore, and that's where I met a new friend. Her name was Elizabeth or Liesbeth as we say in Dutch. We connected right away and she invited me to visit their home to meet her husband. They recently married and were planning to spend their six weeks of Honeymoon in Australia. They needed someone to housesit and asked me. God provided yet another place for me to live. I worked some odd jobs like cleaning offices and translating documents. I had a lot of spare time to pray, read, and contemplate. Then He led me to attend a Full Gospel Church that was started by a couple of Indonesian Dutch families.

It was December by now, and I felt I should start praying for Israel during the Hanukkah season. I invited some friends to come pray with me for Israel. The week before my friends came back from their honeymoon, God spoke very clearly to me to go back to Israel and serve Him there. I had no clue what He wanted me to do in Israel, but when I asked Him when I should leave, He showed me my departure date. It was as if I saw it written, 03-03-03—the 3rd of March 2003.

Once more I set foot in the Promised Land. Little did I know that I was going to be there for the next four years of my life. It was a time of discipleship with Jesus. It started to become clear to me that my life was no longer about pleasing myself but about the Kingdom's purposes of God. Being baptized in the Holy Spirit and fire was the 'game-changer.' Being a good Christian is one thing, but the Christian life levels up when one does not consider our life as our own anymore. Obedience to God, regardless of how it looks or feels, often looks radical! I am writing this for you. Whatever you believe God is asking from you, just do it!

I went to Jerusalem and walked the streets for two days, wondering why God had told me to go back there. The evening of the second day, when I was back in my lodging place, I fervently prayed, asking God to lead me and connect me with some Christians. On the third day I walked the streets again and found myself suddenly inside of the CMJ compound. The Christian Ministry to the Jews is a British Anglican Ministry in the Old City Jerusalem. It was founded by British Evangelical Christians in 1809. The Ministry owns a compound with beautiful ancient buildings across from David's Citadel. The complex consists of a Church, Ministry workers living quarters, a Guesthouse, a Restaurant, a Café, and a Messianic Bookstore. To this day, I believe God's Angels were involved leading me there, as I did not remember noticing the place or walking through its gate. As I wrote before, He led me to the Ministry I ended up working for. So He will lead you to do what He has planned when you pray fervently. There are millions of believers in Christ, but not many completely surrender themselves to His will. *"For many are called, but few are chosen"*, Jesus said in the context of the wedding invitation. Being married to Christ means submitting to His will. Be one of His chosen ones my friend, and you will never have any regrets when you get to Heaven and stand before the Father.

During my short time working at CMJ, I learned a lot. Mind you, I had been such an incredible loner in life, so living and working in a compounded community, wasn't easy for me. I was now faced with my fears of rejection. But God was using the brothers and sisters around me to heal those wounds and shape my character. The work required serving guests who either ate at the Restaurant or stayed in the guesthouse. That is when I met Mrs. Christine Darg, a well-known Healing Evangelist. She has preached the Gospel to the Muslim world for four decades. I was able to attend several of her powerful prayer meetings. God was connecting me with what His will is for the Middle East. I never felt closer to my destiny in God as when I was living in Jerusalem. No city matches Jerusalem. God chose it, our Savior died there and rose again. And He will choose it again for His dwelling place!

*"Yet I have chosen Jerusalem, that My name may be there, and I have chosen David to be over My people Israel." 2 Chronicles 6:6*

King David who was very close to the heart of God, wrote many songs. In one of his Psalms he says, *"For the Lord has chosen Zion, He has desired it for His dwelling place: This is My resting place forever; Here I will dwell, for I have desired it." Psalm 321:13-14*

I never understood how any Christian could read the Bible and not see that Israel is the land He chose for His people to dwell. It is no mistake that after the 2nd World War, the only safe place for surviving Jews was Israel. The prophet Ezekiel spoke of the Holocaust and how the scattered people of God would come back again. *"But you, O mountains of Israel, you shall shoot forth your branches and yield your fruit to My people Israel, for they are about to come." Ezekiel 36:8.* In another place the return of God's people is written, *"For I will take you from among the nations, gather you out of all countries, and bring you into your own land." Ezekiel 36:24*

And of course, the famous passage of the dry bones that will live again:

*"I will put My Spirit in you, and you shall live, and I will place you in your own land. Then you shall know that I, the LORD, have spoken it and performed it," says the LORD.'" Ezekiel 37:14*

# CHAPTER TWELVE

# IF I FORGET YOU, O JERUSALEM

A few weeks after I started working in the CMJ Guesthouse, the USA began to bomb Baghdad in an attempt to topple Saddam Hussein's regime. This happened around March 19th, 2003. Since Israel had been previously attacked by scud missiles from Iraq, we now had become a target again. So we all had to carry gas masks and tape the windows and doors. It was right during the Purim season, the Feast of Esther, where the Jews commemorate the victory God gave them. Our Ministry took extra time to get together and pray. After a week the threats were cleared, and we could put our gas masks away. Israel has gone through many wars ever since it became a Nation. The Assyrian enemies that we read about in the Bible are still in the same geographical locations.

In my free time, when I wasn't serving pilgrims and ministers in the Guesthouse, I would often walk the streets of the Old City Jerusalem. One area special to me is the *Via Dolorosa,* the painful path Jesus walked from being condemned at Pilate's Fortress to His crucifixion at Golgotha. There you will find the stations of the Cross that were marked out by Franciscan monks back in the 14th Century. The Stations are the places where Jesus walked through the city to Golgotha, and key events happened referring to Scripture. The *Via Dolorosa* ends at the location of the *Church of the Holy Sepulcher*. A highly visited place of Christian pilgrimage, as it is believed it was the location of Christ's crucifixion. In later years when I spent more time in Jerusalem, I would often help tourists find their way to the *Church of the Holy Sepulcher*. The old narrow streets of Old City Jerusalem are a maze, and one can get easily lost if you don't know the way. Sometimes I would help Jewish people find their way to the Temple Mount. It was a great honor God bestowed on me. Jews pray, sing and worship at the *Kotel HaMa'aravi*, also known as The Western Wall or Wailing Wall. The place where the glorious Temple of God once stood.

At the Ministry I was working with Christians from Japan, Germany, the USA, and Israel. It was hard work, but I enjoyed it as God used that time to build me up. The way I left the CMJ Ministry is kind of funny when I look back on it now. I had ended up in a conflict of consciousness while working there. The compound had several buildings, and sometimes I would find a Jewish homeless man sleeping on one of the couches inside. He was mostly tolerated, but when I wanted to give him food from our kitchen, I got in trouble with the Management. I honestly don't know who was right and who was wrong in this. They reasoned that Jerusalem has many soup kitchens, and he could go there. I felt he was a poor man sent by God to test our hearts, and I would secretly give him the food that was portioned to me. I was in conflict with myself; not wanting to defy the Management, yet feeling convicted to feed a homeless man. I ended up parting ways with the Ministry. Perhaps it was God's timing.

I was wondering if God wanted me to work for another Ministry or not. I was given the name of an Arab family that had a Church in Nazareth, so I travelled up to see them in the Galilee. I asked the family to pray for me as I was seeking God what to do next. They took me to their parent's Church in Kana, Galilee. It was the place of the wedding where Jesus turned water into wine. They wanted me to share my testimony of how I had an encounter with God that made me follow Jesus. So I shared it in front of the congregation, and someone translated me into Arabic. Some of the Galilee Arab Christians can trace their lineage back to Roman times. They are Arab Israelis living in the Galilee among Jews and Druze. The father of the family brought me to the *Nazareth Village*, an open-air museum where everything is rebuilt as in Jesus's times. I spend some time volunteering with several local people. It is a wonderful outdoor museum where you can step back into the First Century.

After that the family brought me to the home of a former Muslim girl who had become a Christian. I spent about a week with her. She spoke no English, and I quickly learned Arabic from her. When I left Nazareth, the family gave me the address of a home in Haifa where several of their elderly Church members now lived. I didn't think anything of it and felt God wanted me to go back to Holland. However I wanted to stay in Israel so it was a struggle to obey God, but I eventually surrendered to His will.

I flew back to Holland in May, and I was able to work my old Lab Tech job again by the favor of God. Like the year before, I was filling in people's vacation times and was going to be laid off at the end of Summer, in September that year. I prayed all Summer, asking God what He wanted me to do. I listened to my Hebrew Learning CD every day. I repeated the alphabet and the words in the book until I could pronounce them well. One day, near the end of Summer, the Lord dropped on me to contact the Elderly Home in Haifa, the place that the Arab Christian family had written down for me. I searched for the home online and filled out a contact form. The next day I had an email from the Head nurse, saying that they needed volunteers. Then the Lord made it very clear to me that Haifa was the place where I would be going!

# CHAPTER THIRTEEN

# DAYS OF ELIJAH

The Feast of Tabernacles is my favorite Biblical Feast. I won't call it a Jewish Feast because God ordained it for all Tribes and Nations to come to Jerusalem and worship Him. You can read about this in the Book of Zechariah. *"And it shall come to pass that everyone who is left of all the nations which came against Jerusalem shall go up from year to year to worship the King, the LORD of hosts, and to keep the Feast of Tabernacles. And it shall be that whichever of the families of the earth do not come up to Jerusalem to worship the King, the LORD of hosts, on them there will be no rain." Zechariah 14:16-17*

Let me tell you a story I heard from an African believer. His country had been in a drought for years on end. Then God told him he should go to Jerusalem for the Feast of Tabernacles. He had very little money and had to make an arduous journey to get to South Africa, where he could fly to Israel. But he did get on a plane and went to Jerusalem to celebrate and worship God. When he came back to his home country, it started raining for the first time in years! God's word was fulfilled!

When I made my return to Israel to work in the Elderly Home, I took a week in Jerusalem to celebrate the Feast of Tabernacles. I was able to attend the ICEJ* Conference and enjoy great powerful worship with people from all over the world. There is no greater joy than worshipping God with people from all nations, tribes, and tongues. After my week in Jerusalem, I took the bus up to Haifa, where the home was located. God gave me faith to do all this. It was His plan, so I had great peace stepping into the unknown. The Elderly home was started by a Norwegian Ministry in the seventies. Jews who had become believers in Yeshua were often persecuted by their own families. The home provided a safe place for them to live out their faith. Those of you who are familiar with the Ministry called "The Voice of the Martyrs" know that it was started by the Evangelical Romanian Priest, Richard Wurmbrand. He was of Jewish descent. He had endured 14 years of communist imprisonment and torture before he was redeemed by Norwegian Christians. Some of the Romanian Jews in the home that had survived the Holocaust had been Wurmbrand's disciples. You understand that it was a very honorable job God had me do in that home. Sometimes I helped in the kitchen, but I mostly did Nurse-Aid work, helping people get washed and dressed. Some of the residents had Nazi camp numbers tattooed on their wrists. I spent about a year there doing nurse-aid work till the Lord moved me into a different season. It was a year in which I learned a lot about God's grace, His patience, and His tenderness, just by nursing and loving on the elderly. The home also took care of several Arab Christians who had come from Nazareth. I love the Arabic language and how they call the Lord Jesus *"Elrabu Yeshua"*. Hebrew and Arabic are both Semitic languages and have similarities, yet are different at the same time. I took some private Arabic lessons with a lady called ImHanna. In Arabic once you are a parent, you are then called by the name of your oldest child. *Im* means mother in Arabic, and *Abu* means father. In Hebrew, it's *Imma* and *Abba*.

One of the residents, *Sarah,* was a beautiful Christian woman. She first lived independently, but came to our ward after she had broken her hip. Now bound to a wheelchair she often felt frustrated, and she didn't want to join the other residents anymore. But God's grace was there for her. She would call for me when it was her time to take a shower. She had specific ways how she wanted her hair washed, and I would just follow her instructions patiently. The residents had meetings with the staff occasionally in the upstairs assembly room, but she didn't want to attend each time we asked her. One day, as I walked from our workers house to the Residents Home, the earth started shaking under my feet. I thought I had made a misstep, but then realized it was an earthquake. It lasted maybe twenty seconds. When I arrived at the Home, everyone I ran into was talking about it. I was already dressed for my nurse-aid job so I went straight to the ward and walked into Sarah's room to check on her. I loved her very much. I asked her if she felt the earthquake, and then she looked at me quite stunned. "Oh, that's what it was!" And she went on telling me how the nurse had asked if she wanted to come to the meeting but she had refused to go again. Then, right after the nurse left, her wheelchair started rolling back and forth and she felt the Lord saying to her, "Just go!" It was a funny Divine coincidence of events, and that day she let me bring her to the Meeting again.

I had also made friends with a Dutch Jewish resident. She shared many of her life's stories with me as we spoke the same language. It was during her time of hiding in Nazi occupied Holland that she heard the Lord's Prayer on the Dutch resistance radio. She became one of the first Dutch Jewish believers making *Alijah*. When the covenant people of God return to the land of their ancestors, the Land that God promised them, they call it *Alijah*. It wasn't easy in those days to be a Jewish believer in Christ, as most Jews saw it as betrayal to their identity. But nowadays, the number of believers is rapidly growing and they are no longer meeting secretly in homes.

The (Jewish Christian) Congregation I attended was called *Beit Elijahu*, which translates as House of Elijah. It was called that way because not far from the city are the Carmel mountains. It's the place where Elijah had his clash and showdown with the prophets of Baal. It was a Spiritual victory for the true God that people had walked away from. We may think Baal worship is something of the past, but I suggest you look around and see that nothing is new under the sun. Baal worshippers would call on God, yet walk in sin and immorality! A lot of people say they believe in God, but which God are they talking about? Their flesh is the god they serve. Elijah posed his powerful question to the people, *"How long will you falter between two opinions? If Yahweh is God, follow Him; but if Baal, follow him."* *1 Kings 18:21.*

One day while living in Haifa, I went up to Mt Carmel with a fellow worker and read the 18th chapter of 1st Kings out loud. I wanted Elijah's words to resound in the nation of Israel once more because many of them do not acknowledge the true God. Elijah has been referred to in the Bible many times. He is the prophet, the witness that represents God. He appeared together with Moses when Jesus was transfigured into His glory (Matthew 17). And Elijah will appear again as a final witness in the days before Messiah's return. (Revelation 11). He brings the hearts of the Fathers back to the children. (Malachi 4:5-6). If you are reading this and never really decided in your heart who you want to belong to, I suggest you decide it today! Yahweh is the God of Abraham, Isaac, and Jacob. The God of Israel sent His Son, Yeshua ha Mashiach, to teach us the truth and to die for our sins. Call on Yeshua and

He will save you and set you free today! Going back to the days of Elijah is kind of going back to the future. History is prophetic. What has happened will happen again in a different time and setting.

I loved living and working with the elderly in Galilee, but deep down inside I had a longing to go back to Jerusalem. I struggled with this for many months, thinking it was just me. I tried to sacrifice my desire in the name of religious commitment to the place I was working. I had messed up even more because a few months before I had told the Management I would stay there the whole year. That was my plan, but not God's plan for me. I battled the fear of men, yet the Holy Spirit was almost pulling me out of there. I wanted to obey God, but it meant I would greatly disappoint the people I was working for. They expected me to keep my commitment. I battled this for weeks on end. God kept stirring the proverbial nest, yet I didn't make a move. When I worked afternoon-evening shifts, I would often walk several miles in the morning to get to the beach and go for a swim. One day in the middle of that struggle with God's will, I was swimming, when all of a sudden, a big wave came and whacked me right back on the beach. I knew it was the Father's hand, saying, "When will you listen to me?" God knows what language to speak when we need it. I told the management my struggle and how I felt God wanted me to go back to Jerusalem, but no one understood me. They were telling me I was breaking my commitment and even called me rebellious at some point. I don't blame them because it was my fault for committing myself before consulting God. I was a young believer and now had to choose between obeying God or obeying men. I couldn't please both, so I chose to please God and leave the home.

God had been speaking to me about going to an Ulpan to learn Hebrew, and while still in Haifa, I called the School that my German friend had recommended. They had one spot left in the *Aleph* class that was starting in two weeks. I signed up by faith! And the next thing I know I'm on the bus to Jerusalem. I was listening to some Hebrew worship music on my CD "Walkman." As they sang the words, *"Adonay li, lo yirah, ma ya'aseh li adam"* (*The LORD is on my side; I will not fear. What can man do to me?* Psalm 118:6) I just burst into tears. God was with me and man could not harm me. I was going back to my beloved city Jerusalem once more!

*"I was glad when they said to me, "Let us go into the house of the LORD." Our feet have been standing within your gates, O Jerusalem." Psalm 121:1*

*International Christian Embassy Jerusalem

# CHAPTER FOURTEEN

# THE GUESTHOUSE

The Ulpan I attended was called, Ulpan Milah. I loved everything about that School. Classes were in the morning and then lots of homework for the afternoons. As I wrote earlier, I walked by faith. I had no Ministry to provide me with a place to live, so I checked into the Lutheran Guesthouse for a room in their women's dorm. The dorm must have had around 40 bunk beds, it was huge. I felt like a soldier at times, with very little to no privacy, but I was happy and made new friends. The Lord was teaching me that when you are born of the Spirit, you go where He sends you. Even if that doesn't make sense to you or the people around you. (John 3:8) That's the example He gave us. I was a disciple of Him and wanted to follow in His footsteps.

Jesus walked everywhere, so I walked everywhere. It was a two-mile walk to my Hebrew School and probably the same distance to the Church I was attending. One of the Churches called King of Kings was relocating to a new facility. They held Church for years in the YMCA auditorium which I had visited a few times. But now they had purchased and renovated an abandoned cinema in Jerusalem. I was ecstatic to join them! The week they opened there was worship music and singing every day, like when Solomon dedicated the Temple to God. It was a great worship celebration with Paul Wilbur and other Israel-loving musicians.

By the hand of God on me, I immediately got involved in the Church Ministry. I became part of the Intercessory Prayer team, manned the Information Desk on Sundays, and served food on Wednesdays. Between Hebrew School and the Church Ministry, I would be at the Guesthouse. The place has a very interesting history and was built on many layers of ancient Jerusalem history. From its rooftop gardens one can look towards the Temple Mount and see the Mount of Olives. All were reminders of the coming of our Lord! Since I had no School on Fridays and Saturdays, I always kept the Sabbath. I was on a small budget but often felt inspired to cook a big pot of soup and share it with other guests. There was a large communal kitchen and dining area at the Guesthouse. And whoever was there could join the meal. I believe the Lord really liked this because He kept sending guests to the guesthouse who were seeking God. So this Friday meal became a ministry in itself where the Gospel would be shared one way or the other. Sometimes the Lord would send us Orthodox Jews who were lost in tradition and were seeking deliverance. By this time the Lord had sent one or two American Evangelists that would join me. I never even tried to imitate anything Church-like, but somehow the Lord always showed up. We would break bread together, pray, and share our testimonies. It was as if Jesus was glad to visit us and I often felt His presence so tangibly. It was as if we had become part of history in the present. One time some Irish backpackers came and told us that as they walked the streets of Jerusalem, they felt God was calling them, but they didn't know what to do. And then He led them to our Guesthouse! I was very humbled, as you can imagine. But like any good and beautiful ministry with Jesus, some type of Judas had to come in. I would rather not waste too many words on this story, but someone was trying to betray me. Some people believe that Christians try to convert Jews and take away their identity. They feel threatened and try to stop Christians from sharing the Gospel. One night this young man, whom I assumed was an agent of the anti-missionaries, had come in again. It was on *erev shabbat*, just when I was about to serve my soup. He pretended to be interested in Christianity, but I knew something was off. There were several believers that evening. I didn't want him to be part of our meal in which we would share about the Lord. In distress I went down into the basement where my dorm bed was. I covered myself in a blanket and prayed, "Lord, that man is here. You know who he is. What do I do?" And clear as a voice from Heaven I heard the Lord say to me, "My betrayer was among Me." I was stunned by this answer but felt strengthened and had peace. I was not to be afraid of anyone. My fate was in God's hands. I decided to be loving and kind to any man who joined our meal. I had to trust God with my time in Israel. It wasn't the first time that a Christian's visa was being revoked. I knew an Asian Christian who was taken by the religious establishment and put on an airplane back to his home country.

I will share a few other stories of my time in the Lutheran Guesthouse. As I said earlier, the Lord kept sending people to the Guesthouse who needed to hear the truth, or sometimes women who needed healing. God knew I lived in a 'borrowed home', so He brought anyone He wanted. I ministered to several hurting women, and sometimes even solved issues between women that were at odds. God had given me the wisdom and authority to do so. I never decided that on my own, it was given to me from Heaven. At any time when the anointing flows, the enemy will come and try to stop it. So, that serpent of old sent one of his agents to throw me off. This time it was a woman who had checked in as a guest and stayed in the dorms as well. She seemed to be completely controlled by a demonic spirit. At night she would stand next to my bed and curses would come out of her mouth. I could feel the presence of demons oppressing me. I would pray, but it took me hours battling in the Spirit, and my peace would not return to me. After two nights of the same I found out that she had also given my food (that was stored in the shared fridge) to the street cats! I had to go see my Pastor, so I went to the Church that morning before I entered School. I had fallen out of fellowship over a doctrinal difference, but I repented of it and my Pastor prayed for me. I went to my Hebrew class after that and then returned to the Guesthouse. The women's dorm was in an underground layer of Jerusalem, with walls of old Jerusalem stone. The arched-shaped door was set with a heavy metal door. When it was my time to go to sleep, the demonized woman wasn't there yet. I decided to apply the Blood of Jesus by faith on the metal door and stone arch frame. There was a little night light above the door, but the dorm itself was dark. There were no windows except an escape shaft with a ladder to get up to level ground. My bed was several yards away from the door. And I fell asleep on my bottom bunk bed. I woke up around midnight to the sound of the old metal door opening. As I looked, I saw the witch woman standing in front of the door, but she couldn't walk through! She stood there for a long time, but I decided to go back to sleep. The next morning, I could see her bed was untouched. God had given me the victory in Jesus! When I came back from my Hebrew class that day, the Manager of the Guesthouse told me the lady had come back but checked out and left. What spiritual lessons I learned in Jerusalem. It would take another book to describe everything that I learned there. People came and tried to deceive me with twisted kind of Gospels. One guest, who sat with me while I was eating my vegetarian spaghetti, started talking about the raw food diet. He shared with me how Biblical it was to eat raw foods and he went on so convincingly until I felt guilty eating my processed spaghetti. I just let him talk and decided I was losing the argument anyway. When he was done talking, I simply said, "So you are preaching the Gospel of the Good Food!" And that was the end of that.

At some point in time, the Friday's Soup Ministry came to an end and I had to move out of the guesthouse where I had stayed for long periods of time. The Guesthouse had changed Management and they wanted me and another long-term guest to leave. They told us we needed to leave by Sunday. It was Friday morning, so I had three days to find another place to stay. I was really longing for more privacy, but couldn't afford to rent an apartment. Of course I prayed, but I felt a little distressed about it. On Friday mornings I often went to the Church to help assemble bulletins for Sunday's Service. I asked in the group if anyone knew of a place to stay. One lady said she rented a room in the Old City, and believed there was another room available. After we were done with the bulletins, I walked with her to the house she stayed. Like many a place in Old Jerusalem, they wanted more rent money then I thought I could afford. I told the family that I needed to think and pray about it and left. Back in the Guesthouse I desperately cried out to God what I should do. I loved the idea of having some privacy, but it was more then I wanted to pay. I prayed and prayed, asking God if this was the place I should rent. And then I felt God's presence come, and randomly opened my Bible. My eyes fell on the following verses. *"Here I will dwell, for I have desired it. I will abundantly bless her provision; I will satisfy her poor with bread." (Psalm 132:14-15).* Those words were lifted of the page, and surrounded by a heavenly light. It went straight into my Spirit like a piece of bread and I ate it. I knew God was giving me faith He would provide for the dwelling. And so, by Divine revelation, I was able to rent a small room in the courtyard area of an Arab Christian family. It was such a blessed place for me as I finally had some privacy and uninterrupted sleep!

I was a disciple of Jesus and considered that a great privilege. He was always so near and close. I lived a sober and simple life out of a suitcase for years, yet I was rich in Christ. It wasn't easy or romantic, but Jesus was there, and I was happy because I was doing the work of the Kingdom. I spent hours and days in intercession when I had breaks from Hebrew School. When I rented the little room with the Arab family I had a lot of alone time, as there were no more guests and no sleeping quarters to share. I remember I read every prophetic book from the Bible out loud. From Isaiah till Malachi. It's amazing how much the Word of God makes sense when everything else is turned off. I had no TV, cellphone, or Internet. And being in the very country where the prophets lived and were stoned, the Holy Spirit, who saw it all, connected me with the past in the present. To me, as a Christian Zionist, there was no greater fulfillment than to live, pray, and worship God in the very city He called His own.

*"Thus says the LORD: 'I will return to Zion, and dwell in the midst of Jerusalem." Zechariah 8:3*

Sometimes I joined Christine Darg in her Prayer Ministry. She has taken groups up on the Walls of Jerusalem for years. (Yes, you can literally walk on the walls of the Old City) I was simply a vessel for the Lord, and a watchman on the walls for the three years I was there. When I left, I was certain that the Lord already had other prayer warriors in place.

*"I have set watchmen on your walls, O Jerusalem; They shall never hold their peace, day or night. You who make mention of the Lord, do not keep silent, and give Him no rest till He establishes and till He makes Jerusalem a praise in the earth." Isaiah 62:6-7*

Thank you for sticking around this long, joining me on my journey through the Middle East. I hope you understand that the Crossroads and ancient paths are really about the Messiah Yeshua. He is the only One that will give you rest.

*"Stand at the crossroads and look; ask for the ancient paths, ask where the good way is, and walk in it, and you will find rest for your souls." Jeremiah 6:16 NIV*

*Yeshua said, "Come to me, all you who labor and are heavy laden, and I will give you rest." Matthew 11:28*

# CHAPTER FIFTEEN

# EVENTFUL JERUSALEM STORIES

Life is never dull in Jerusalem. The city is the pinnacle of three world religions, so you can imagine the warfare you have to wade through to get something done. I learned that to do anything, I had to PRAY first. A simple thing like making an international phone call from a landline would never work until I prayed myself through the hindrances. This was before cell phones and internet calls. I would have an international calling card with limited minutes. I would call my beloved mother in Holland to let her know I was still alive and well.

I haven't written much about the Israeli Defense Forces, but I will now. As you probably know, since Israel's rebirth in 1948, it has been in a constant state of war and hostilities. There are always *chayalim* (soldiers) everywhere. And the IDF usually keeps soldiers stationed near the gates of the Old City. To understand this following 'eventful' story, I have to give you a little history first. In the late 1990's and early 2000's there were several bus bombings and suicide attacks carried out by either Hamas, Fatah, PIJ, or other Arab terrorists. As a result of that, when you enter a public building in Jerusalem, you will encounter a soldier or security guard scanning and checking your bags and walking you through a metal detector.

One time I was with some friends, and we were having lunch at the patio of CMJ's Restaurant. The place is not far from the Old City's walls and the famous Yaffa Gate. Someone else joined us a little later and said that the IDF had everything blocked off near Yaffa Gate because of a bomb scare. Now, you think we'd all be in terror, but we simply kept on eating our lunches and chatting away. Half an hour later or so, another friend came through the gate of the compound. He walked on with his suitcase that had a giant hole blasted in it. He said, "The IDF shot my suitcase!" And when I realized that his suitcase was the bomb scare, I started laughing like crazy! It turned out that our friend, who was about to leave for the Airport, had left his suitcase with some friends near the gate. We're not sure what happened, but the suitcase was abandoned at some point and therefore it became a suspicious object. When our friend opened his suitcase, his clothes and cowboy boots were holed through! Of course, he didn't think it was funny, but I never laughed so much as then. Roy, if you ever read my book, please forgive me for laughing at your destroyed suitcase. I appreciated you so much for coming to Israel and sharing about Yeshua with the people, despite the oppositions you faced. To me, the shot-through suitcase fitted your cowboy lifestyle and you left Israel with a blast!

I met some wonderful fine Christians in Jerusalem who came to serve the Lord and His people. One of them was an Irish woman, Cara, who was of my age. She served in several Ministries and had a warm heart. She had an energetic and bubbly personality. We didn't see each other every Sunday but one time we were sitting together in Church when a Minister called Sid Roth had come from the USA. He was sharing about miracles God had done while he was in Galilee. He learned that the Jewish people saw that Yeshua was the Messiah by ministering healing miracles to them. As he was sharing several testimonies, he then went in the same Spirit saying that people were being healed right now in our sanctuary. He mentioned several ailments by name and then asked people to stand up if they felt the Lord had touched them and healed them. Cara, who was sitting right beside me, stood up, and in my astonishment, I nearly pulled her down. "What?! He healed you of what?" But when Sid Roth asked her what the Lord healed her of, she said a toothache! And she sat down. I looked at her, still astonished. I couldn't believe that a miracle happened right next to me and I didn't feel a thing! She then whispered to me how she had an aching molar all day, but after Sid Roth ministered it was gone. God must have shaken His head at me being so surprised. I then remembered my first encounter with a miracle of healing, which was exactly that of a toothache as well!

During my work at CMJ and attending the Church there, I had made some Arab friends. They both were in their early thirties like me. He worked as a cook sometimes for CMJ and his wife was taking care of their little children. Her parents lived near the ninth Station of the Cross right in the middle of the Christian Quarter. King David said it so well, *"Jerusalem is built as a city compact together."* To find my friend's parents' house, I needed to remember which turn to take and when. Forget about Street signs, they don't exist there. If I hadn't visited for quite some time, I would not remember how to find their home. They were so kind; they would send their son to meet me at her husband's restaurant and he would walk me to their house. Arab families are extremely hospitable. I don't remember not eating food in their house. It didn't matter if you just ate lunch or Dinner, you had to eat something!

One time in a meeting, I heard an older Arab Christian speaking Aramaic, the language Jesus spoke. It sounds so beautiful. Together with a few other Christians, we made some friends with a couple of Arab Christians from Bethlehem. We had gone on several outreach trips there, and they would invite us to come to their homes.

Most Arab Christians grew up in the Eastern Orthodox Church. These guys were telling us a story, of how a man came from Egypt and preached the Gospel to them in a community hall. And they all got so convicted of their sin, they were crying and laying on the floor. Jesus met them there and they surrendered their lives. They felt the presence of God so strong that some of them became instant Evangelists themselves and started preaching the Gospel to their Muslim friends. They were bold and courageous. One of the guys ran a weaving and clothing factory in the area. He said they would get attacked by their people because they used to make T-shirts for the IDF. I'm just painting a picture here so you have an idea about life in Israel. Bethlehem used to be under Israeli control and the Christian community was pretty large. Since the control was given to the P.A. most Christians have moved away because of Muslim hostilities. One time when we were there on outreach, we experienced these hostilities firsthand. May God forgive them, for they know not what they do.

On Fridays all buses stop running around 1-2 p.m. for the Sabbath. I had forgotten all about it so I had to walk home one day from Bethlehem to Jerusalem. I walked for two hours in the heat, hiking uphill approaching Jerusalem. But I felt so privileged I could walk these ancient paths knowing that God was with me. Jerusalem also hosts Christians of other backgrounds, Russian Orthodox for example. They too have had a long-time presence in the Holy City. I had never met any of them until one time. As I was walking back from *Ulpan* into the Old City, I saw an elderly nun walking with heavy bags in both hands, so I offered to help her. She spoke broken English but was a precious woman of God. As we walked through the Old City's *HaShaar haChadash* (New Gate) she went on to tell me how she had lived in the same place in Jerusalem for fifty years. I was amazed, and went on to ask her how it was during the Six-Day War? (This was the war in 1967 when the IDF captured Jerusalem from Jordanian rule.) Then my little nun friend said with a strong Russian accent, "There was no bread." And just as she said it, we walked by one of the oldest pita bread bakeries in the city. I thought, "Wow, how does God do that?" It was as if our conversation was staged for a movie. I started to be more appreciative of my daily bread, that's for sure. I took God's history lessons seriously.

Nuns have a special place in my life. At some point in life, I wanted to be one, but God said no. I cried, but then I got over it. You need to know your calling and apply wisdom when you are full of zeal. I learned that the hard way, but *"His rod and staff comforted me."* I devoted ten years of my single life to serving the Lord, and then when I was forty, I got married.

In my Hebrew class, there were two nuns dressed in white and one Franciscan monk. Mind you, we had students from all layers of society. There were Jewish immigrants from Romania, Russia, the USA and France, Arab students who needed Hebrew to study at university, along with a bunch of us Christians. I became friends with one of the nuns, Maria. I have known very few people in whom the love of Christ radiates through their whole being with purity and serenity. Maria was one of them. She was also the shy type, and I'm not. Perhaps that was a good formula for our friendship. In our break times from class, we would always share things the Lord was doing in our lives. Sometimes we shared revelations we had from reading the Scriptures with new Hebrew understanding. It was in the days when I lived very frugal on a few shekels a day. And sometimes I would come home after Class and find a couple of apples in my bag, or a fifty shekel note! I never knew where those surprise findings in my daypack came from, but I have a feeling my nun friend Maria had something to do with it.

When I would come out of school, I usually went straight home to the little room I rented. It would take about thirty minutes to walk back to the Old City. You have to understand that people from all kinds of ages, religions, and ethnicities live in Jerusalem. To see someone dressed in an *Abaya* (Arab long gown) was nothing new for me. Jewish orthodox men pretty much dress in the same black suits, and some of the Karaites wear all-white gowns. One day I stood waiting at the pedestrian crossing at the end of Yaffa Street and *Shivtei Yisrael*. It's a busy zebra crossing with traffic lights where you cross over to enter the Old City. There were maybe twenty people waiting for the light to turn green. And then I saw a man who looked like an ancient prophet, someone like Moses or Elijah. He was wearing ancient-looking robes of terra-colored material. He had a long wooden stick in his hand, long greyish-white hair, and a full beard. I was so stunned; I couldn't believe my eyes! Up until this day, I don't know if I saw him in the natural or saw him in the Spirit. Or worse, if I had gone crazy! But there it is. In hindsight I thought, "I should have followed him to see where he went." But in that moment, there was such an impressed fear of God on me, that I wouldn't have dared it. I didn't carry a cellphone, so there was no picture-taking either, just a picture in my mind. I believe God lifted the veil and showed me they will return and witness about the Messiah soon!

# CHAPTER SIXTEEN

## GROWING FAITH

The little room I rented with the Arab Christian family was precious to me. Upon entering there was one single bed, two classic chairs upholstered with dark red fabric, a writing table and chair, a fridge and a sink. Then at the end of the room there was a stand-in kitchen of about 6 square feet. The toilet with a makeshift shower above it was even smaller than that. I would wash my clothes by hand in the sink and dry them on a line in the patio area. Water inside the Old City is full of limestone so you always felt soapy even after rinsing off. But none of that mattered to me. I was happy with my little room of privacy. I don't know how I did this, but I managed to keep a little Sabbath Bible study in that room. Usually, four to six of my friends would come.

On Friday mornings I would walk a long way to shop at the *Ma-hane Yehudah* (outdoor Farmers market). It's one of my favorite places in Jerusalem. You can find any type of Middle Eastern food there. And many vendors are calling out what they're selling with the price. Depending on my budget I would buy a couple of pita breads, some vegetables, and freshly made hummus. One Saturday morning, as I was preparing for my friends to come, I was thinking of saving some of my bread. Knowing I had no money left to buy new bread in the days to come. But somehow, when we were done with our Bible study, I decided to put all the food I had on the table. I halved all the pita breads and everyone ate of it. We enjoyed our fellowship and prayed for each other's needs. When they all left, I gathered up the pieces. To my astonishment, I saw that there was the exact amount of pita left than what I had started with! The Lord had multiplied my food!

That was the year when the Lord would not let me return to Holland in the Summer. Remember, I would work in the Summer and provide for my missions. Now He was teaching me that He would provide for me. He did this in a very profound way. The Christian Friends of Israel Ministry had a free Library. I would go there once a week and check out teaching tapes from Derek Prince. I probably listened to a hundred of them. I never read any books during that season of my life, but wanted to keep my Spirit undefiled by reading the Bible only. On one of my visits to the library, however, I felt the Lord wanted me to get Lydia Prince's book *Appointment in Jerusalem*. It was Winter by this time, and I would sit curled up in the dark red chair with a blanket on me. My room was not heated, but the book was so intriguing to me that I didn't care. After a few nights of reading, I finished the book and closed it. Then the Lord's presence filled my room, and He let me know that He would always provide for those He called. That's when the faith journey for food and rent began. I didn't have any type of home-front support network, but God didn't need it. He simply sent His "ravens"! Now, it wasn't always easy to trust God to feed me. You may think I was a woman of faith, and that's what I thought too, until it came down to that level of trust. I was shaken to the core. I believe The Father wanted a deep relationship with me. This depth could only come through much prayer, tears, and absolute dependence on Him. Month after month I had no idea where the next rent money would come from. But God always came through. I started to grow in faith. I would take my last shekels to the Market, buy my food, and drop my left-over coins into the cups of the homeless. My money was gone, but I was full of joy. Sometimes I walked on clouds of faith, and at other times I was tested in different ways.

Our Church would often have tea and cakes after the service. Sunday is a work day in Israel, so our service started at 5 p.m. and was done around 7 p.m. I saw one of my friends after service and walked up to her. She was at a table selling home-baked cakes for a shekel a piece. We chatted a little and then she said, "Do you want a cake?" I told her that I didn't have a shekel. That was true, but she didn't know I was dead poor, and perhaps she thought I didn't carry money to Church. But then she said, "I'll buy you one." And so, I picked out my cake. A delicacy I hadn't eaten in a while. I wrapped it in a napkin and decided to eat it at home. Walking the miles-long Yaffa Street back to the Old City, I would always see a couple of homeless men holding up their plastic cups for coins. I knew their faces and the places they sat. However, this time I saw a homeless man I had never seen before. He had half-long dark hair and a dark beard. His clothes didn't look too raggedy, but I could tell he was in need. I first passed him thinking I had nothing to give. But then I remembered my slice of cake. And so I walked a few steps back and gave it to him and said, "Here, this is for you." He smiled with a lit-up face and said, "Thank you." As I walked along, the joy of the Lord surrounded me. Angels came and I started singing praises to God. Walking the streets of Jerusalem, I had given my all to Yeshua because He gave it all for us. I never knew if this mysterious homeless man was the Lord, an Angel, or just a man. I walked that street every day, but I never saw him again.

*"You have tested my heart; You have visited me in the night; You have tried me and have found nothing; I have purposed that my mouth shall not transgress." Psalm 17:3*

# CHAPTER SEVENTEEN

# DEPARTURE

Flights from Israel bound for Amsterdam often leave in the early morning hours. The shared taxi ride from Jerusalem to Tel Aviv Airport is always fun. Driving to and through the neighborhood hills of Jerusalem you get to see places you never knew existed. People from all walks of life pile into the van and suitcases pile up in the back of the van. Every time you think to yourself, "O man, we're full", the driver has yet to make another stop. Israeli *Sherut* drivers are miracle workers. They can fit more people and luggage in their vans than naturally possible. When you get to the Airport in Israel there is an extensive security protocol you will be subjected to. Maybe it was more so for me, because traveling alone as a woman in the Middle East is not a very common thing. One early morning on inspecting my suitcase, a stern security guard asked me if I had anything in there about Israel. I thought for a second and then I pulled my Bible out and jokingly said, "This is full of stories about Israel." It made the young man smile. Another time when leaving my beloved Israel, I cried so hard on the plane I felt inconsolable. Then I opened my Bible and read the following words, *"Those who sow in tears shall reap in joy. He who continually goes forth weeping, bearing seed for sowing, shall doubtless come again with rejoicing, bringing his sheaves with him." Psalm 126:5-6*

That was it. God said I would come again rejoicing. And I did! I went back and forth between Israel and Holland for about four years.

One of the times I flew back to Holland I was just exhausted. After being up all night, I boarded the plane in the early morning hours. Once I got in my seat, I pulled my scarf over my face and dozed off. The next thing I knew was that I woke up from the clonking sound of the airplane's wheels hitting the tarmac. We arrived in Holland. I had slept the whole flight as if God had taken me to Heaven. My time in Jerusalem came to an end in 2007. It was glorious and a great joy to be with Christians from all over the world. But it was through trials and tribulations that God created these gemstones, *the hidden riches of secret places*. It would have been selfish to keep all these treasured stories to myself. I never felt my time in Israel was completed or finished. But I came to believe overtime that God wanted to leave it that way; open ended.

A few years after I married, my husband and I made a trip to Israel. It was now 2014, seven years after I left. It was very exciting to show my husband all the places I loved in Jerusalem. We also took a tour around the Galilee. I was hoping we would find a ministry we could work for and stay, but God didn't want us to stay that time. He did give us a blessed gift before we left because we found out six weeks later that I was pregnant with our son Joshua!

This book is coming to an end. Thank you for joining me in walking the ancient paths. I hope you enjoyed the journey and learned that walking with God is the way to find rest for your soul. Yeshua said of Himself, *"I am the way, the truth and the life." (John 14:6)*. My prayer for you is that you will make it to the Promised Land one day. If God puts the desire in your heart to go, He will make the way for you. Just believe it and make preparations for your journey.

*"Blessed is the man whose strength is in You, whose heart is set on pilgrimage. As they pass through the Valley of Baca, they make it a spring; the rain also covers it with pools. They go from strength to strength; each one appears before God in Zion." Psalm 84:5-7*

# ENDNOTE

The defamation of Israel and the Jews is not a new thing. *"The Lion of the tribe of Judah"* gave us a clear message that we should always take care of His people. God's Word also tells us that we will be judged on how we treat His people.

*"For behold, in those days and at that time, when I bring back the captives of Judah and Jerusalem, I will also gather all nations, and bring them down to the Valley of Jehoshaphat; And I will enter into judgment with them there on account of My people, My heritage Israel, whom they have scattered among the nations; they have also divided up My land. They have cast lots for My people, have given a boy as payment for a harlot, and sold a girl for wine, that they may drink." Joel 3:1-3*

Biblical truth is the best compass when it comes down to navigating the current events in the Middle East. In Matthew 25 Yeshua talks about the same judgment that will come for all nations on behalf of what we have done to *His brethren*. In the 20th Century the Jews were persecuted, defamed, and murdered in Europe, the USSR, and the Middle East. Now in our days, the 21st

Century, Ezekiel's prophesy has been fulfilled; the Jews are back in their own Land. However, when Israel defends herself against her enemies, they still get persecuted, defamed, and murdered. Satan hates God's covenant people with a passion, but we know his days are numbered. Soon our Jewish Messiah will return, and He will *"rule the Nations with a rod of iron" (Psalm 2:9, Revelation 19:15)*

I hope to return to the Promised Land with my family one day. I am holding on to the Isaiah 8:18 promise. Many Christians believe that God will 'rapture' us away before the Great Tribulation of the last days. I believe Yeshua needs us in Mount Zion and will keep us from the hour of trial when we keep His word and persevere. (Revelation 3:7-13) Let's be the faithful remnant, the Joel 2 army on whom the Lord can count!

*"And I will show wonders in the heavens and the earth: Blood and fire and pillars of smoke. The sun shall be turned into darkness, and the moon into blood, before the coming of the great and awesome day of the LORD. And it shall come to pass that whoever calls on the name of the LORD shall be saved. For in Mount Zion and in Jerusalem there shall be deliverance, as the LORD has said, among the remnant whom the LORD calls. Joel 2:32*

**Christian Organizations in the Middle East (mentioned in the book)**

CMJ (Christian Ministry to the Jews)
www.cmj-israel.org

Jerusalem Channel (Christine Darg)
www.jerusalemchannel.tv

International Christian Embassy Jerusalem
www.icej.org

King of Kings Community
www.kkcj.org

# ACKNOWLEDGMENTS

I couldn't have done anything in life solely by myself. Many thanks go out to:

My husband, who graciously has given me the space to write this book, and then edited it as well. He has been a faithful provider for our family, so I can be free to be who I am in God. He keeps me laughing when I get too serious, happy when I'm sad, and lifts me up when I'm down. *Two are better than one...and a threefold cord is not quickly broken. Eccl. 4:9-12.* Chris, you know how much I love you!

My father, who has always been supportive of my travels and undertakings. He never discouraged me in anything, but let me explore my talents and calling in life. On my many returns from foreign places, he was faithfully there to pick me up from the train station. My father was the one who told me to get my old Diaries out and write this book. Thank you Pap, you're the best Dad I could ever wish for!

My mother, who would always take me back into her home when I would return from travels and missions. She would pamper me with my favorite foods, a comfortable bed and do my laundry.

My mother has taught me to serve and do it without complaining! Her love for me has pierced many times the hardness of my heart. She has been the most prominent person in my life to instill faith and devotion to God. I love you to eternity Mom!

My sister, who has often provided me with much-needed new clothes after my finances were drained. She has also made me part of her family for all the years I was still single. She has been my best friend forever. Through various times and seasons in life she never stopped loving me. Hilda, I miss you terribly at times, but I love you always my sweet sister!

Friends from all over the world who have helped me to get to my destinations. Not to forget the people of the Middle East who have gone above and beyond to guide me, feed me and help me.

Father God, Who never left me or forsook me. He has been incredibly patient with me all these years. He gave me many gifts, talents, favors, and privileges in life just because He loves me. No other words can describe my gratitude to You, Father. I love you with my all my heart, all my soul and all my mind. I can't wait to spend eternity with You!

# Also by Mirjam Johnson

# ABOUT THE AUTHOR

Mirjam has been a missionary for about twenty years. She loves talking about the Kingdom of God and helping people find freedom in Christ.

Her passion is to see the people of God walk in the power of the Holy Spirit. She finds it her calling to raise an Army of believers to conquer the earth for Christ.

Mirjam lives with her husband and son in Chattanooga, Tennessee. Besides home-making, ministry, and writing, she likes to pioneer new things and use her creative abilities to reach people around the world.